Why I Teach

Why I Teach

PETER G. BEIDLER

02 03 04 05 06 KWF 10 9 8 7 6 5 4 3 2 1

ISBN: 0-7407-2209-3

Library of Congress Control Number: 2001053346

ATTENTION: SCHOOLS AND BUSINESSES

Andrews McMeel books are available at quantity discounts with bulk purchase for educational, business, or sales promotional use. For information, please write to: Special Sales Department, Andrews McMeel Publishing, 4520 Main Street, Kansas City, Missouri 64111.

INTRODUCTION

This little book began nearly twenty years ago when I was named national Professor of the Year by the Carnegie Foundation and CASE—Council for Advancement and Support of Education. As a result of that award the editors of the *Alumni Magazine Consortium* invited me to write a short essay. They published it as "Why Do I Teach?"

A year later the editors of *Reader's Digest* read the essay, liked it, and reprinted it in somewhat condensed form, under the new title I suggested, "Why I Teach." It received wide readership in that form and was translated into at least eight languages for international editions of *Reader's Digest*.

Many years later, when I was teaching as a Fulbrighter in China, one of my students asked me if I was the Peter G. Beidler who wrote "Why I Teach." I owned up and asked how he had heard of it. He said it was in his English-language textbook. He and his classmates had been asked to analyze its language for an assignment in contemporary English usage.

And many years after that, in the late fall of 2000, I got out of the cyberblue an e-mail from a young teacher in mainland China. She asked me if I was the Professor Beidler who wrote "Why I Teach." I owned up again. Then she told me that when she graduated from college she was good enough in English that she had a choice of becoming an English teacher or going into international business.

Torn, she went back and reread my "Why I Teach" from one of her college textbooks and decided, on the spot, to become a teacher. She said she had no regrets whatsoever about her choice, and now she was teaching my essay to others in her own English classes. Did I know, she asked, that my essay was required reading for perhaps a couple million college English students in China each year?

I didn't know that but of course was pleased to learn that the essay was still in circulation. I told the folks at Lehigh University's office of media relations, and they wrote something up and sent it to *Time* magazine. In the early spring of 2001 *Time* published a very short notice about the readership of my essay in China.

An editor at Andrews McMeel saw the *Time* piece and asked to see a copy. A few months later she said that Andrews McMeel wanted to make a little book of my essay. Was I interested? I said I was. Although I was a college teacher, my words, now somewhat revised and expanded, might have meaning for teachers at other levels and might help others decide what to do with their lives—especially in this era of disillusioned teachers and looming teacher shortages. I am pleased to have *Why I Teach* made available, once again.

Incidentally, I never did become an administrator. I have more important work to do.

"Why do you teach, Pete?" My friend asked the question when I told him that I didn't want to be considered for a university administrative position. He was puzzled that I did not want to take what was obviously a step toward what all American boys are taught to want when they grow up, money and power.

I told him that as a teacher

I had both a decent salary

and the only kind of

power worth having,

the power to change lives.

"Besides," I said,
"I like my job in part
because no administrator
has ever told me how to
teach or what to teach or
how to treat students. Why
would I want to be an administrator
cut off from the only kind of power that
matters in a university?"

But he had
stopped listening,
so I stopped talking.
I was not satisfied with
that answer anyhow. His
question got me thinking, though.
This little book is an extended answer to
the question "Why do you teach, Pete?"

Certainly I don't
teach because teaching
comes naturally to me. I was
about the quietest kid in class all
through high school and college. My
teachers just couldn't get me to talk.
The last thing I wanted to do for a
career was stand in front of a
group of people and jabber.

And certainly I don't
teach because teaching
is easy for me. Teaching is the
most difficult of the various ways I have
attempted to earn my living: bulldozer
mechanic, carpenter, temporary
college administrator, writer.

For me, teaching is a red-eye, sweaty-palm, sinking-stomach profession. Red-eye because I never feel ready to teach, no matter how late I stay up the night before preparing for class. Sweaty-palm because I'm always nervous before I walk into that classroom, sure that I will be found out this time. Sinking-stomach because I walk out of the classroom an hour later convinced that I was even more stuttering and bumbling than usual.

Nor do I teach because I think I know answers, or because I know a body of information I feel driven to share.

Sometimes I am amazed that my students actually take notes on what I say in class.

Why, then, *do* I teach?

Well, I teach because
I like the pace of the academic calendar.

I like it that twice a year,
whether I am done or not, the semester ends.

I get to turn in my grades, clean off my desk,
and make a fresh start in a new semester,
unshackled from the mistakes and problems
of the past one.

I teach because
    June, July, and August
        offer an opportunity for
            my own three R's—
                reflection, research, and writing—
        all ingredients in my recipe for teaching.

I teach because
I like the freedom to make my own
mistakes, to learn my own lessons, to
stimulate myself and my students. As a
teacher, I am my own boss. If I want my
first-year composition students to learn
to write by creating in the course of the
semester their own writing textbook, who
is to say I may not? Such courses may be
colossal failures, but I can learn from my
colossal failures.

Unlike most professionals,
I get to erase my mistakes
twice a year, wash the blackboard,
and start off on a whole new
set of trials and the errors
that come with them.

I teach because I like to ask questions that students must struggle to answer. The world is full of right answers to bad questions. Teaching, I sometimes brush up against good questions.

I teach
because I
like to learn.

Take the comma out of the question

"Why do you teach, Pete?"

and you get a better question,

"Why do you teach Pete?"

I teach Pete because Pete gets as stale as ·
day-old beer if Pete stops learning.

I stay alive as a teacher
only as long as I am learning.

One of the major
discoveries of my
professional life
is that I teach
best not what I know,
but what I want to learn.

I teach because

I enjoy finding ways
within an ivory-tower
profession to get myself
and my students
out of the ivory tower
and into the world.
I once taught a course called
"Self-Reliance in a Technological Society."

My fifteen students read Emerson and Thoreau and Huxley. They kept journals. They wrote term papers.

But we also set up a corporation, borrowed money from a bank, purchased a run-down house on nearby Vernon Street, and practiced self-reliance by renovating it. At the end of the semester we sold the house, repaid our loan, paid our capital gains taxes, and distributed the profits among the fifteen students.

Certainly this was not your average English course.

But fifteen future lawyers, accountants, dentists, and businesspeople suddenly found themselves reading *Walden* with fresh eyes.

Now they knew why Thoreau went to the woods, why he built his own cabin, and why he felt so good about the experiment that he wanted to tell the world about it.

They also
knew why,
in the end,
he left both
the cabin
and the woods.

He had tasted the waters of Walden Pond.
It was time to move on to other nectars.

I teach because teaching gives me many nectars to taste, many books to read, and many ivory and real-world towers to discover.

Teaching gives me pace and variety and challenge and the opportunity to keep on learning.

I teach
for all those reasons,

but they are
not the most
important reasons
why I teach.

I teach
because of
Vicky.

My first doctoral student, Vicky, was an energetic and enthusiastic young bubble who had trouble seeing past the thrill of literature to the rigor of academic scholarship. But she plugged away at her dissertation on a nameless, little-known fourteenth-century poet. She hammered out some articles and sent them off to learned journals. She got a good job at a good university in Atlanta. She got involved in fund raising for her university.

The last I heard from her
she was being considered for
a college presidency. I had little
to do with her success as an
academic, but I was there,
grinning like an idiot,
when she graduated.

Another reason is

"Stan,"

the Americanized name
of a student I taught
as a Fulbrighter in China.

During China's cultural revolution Stan watched his father be executed, was sent to the countryside to be educated by illiterate pig farmers, taught himself English with a dictionary and a couple of Victorian novels, and eventually became an English teacher at the Chinese university where I taught for a year.

I was eventually able
to bring him to Lehigh University,
where he earned his Ph.D.

He is now back in China,
teaching brilliantly.

Another reason is
Jeanne.

Jeanne
ran away
from college,
but some of her classmates
brought her back because they
wanted her to see the end of
the self-reliance house project.
I was there when she came back.

I was there when she told me, years later,
why she ran away that semester and how
much she needed to come back to my course.

It is not, she said, that she was
rebuilding the house on Vernon Street.

It was that she was rebuilding Jeanne.

The last I heard
she had finished
her law degree
and went on
to become a
civil-rights lawyer.

Another reason is
George,
one of the brightest
students I have ever had.

He started as an engineering student, then switched to English because he decided he liked people better than things, because he was more interested in personalities than in hypotenuses, because he preferred worrying with the stress fractures in people than with the stress fractures in concrete beams. He stayed at Lehigh for a master's degree.

The last I heard
George was
teaching English in
a junior high school,
shaping people
rather than bridges.

Another reason is
Jacqui,
a cleaning woman who knew
more by intuition than most
of us ever learn by analysis.

We chatted about this and that while she was emptying my wastepaper basket. Then one day we chatted longer over a cup of coffee while she was on her break. This woman who dropped out of high school became my teacher.

She was amazed that a professor was interested in what she knew, amazed that I wondered why anyone so smart would be emptying my waste basket. She told me that even work like that had its rewards.

Later Jacqui quit her job and went back to finish high school. I am not sure what happened after that. But I know, by intuition, that she is okay. And I know that she is no longer emptying other people's waste baskets. She can't be.

These are the

real reasons I teach,

these people who

grow and change

in front of my eyes.

Being a teacher
is being present at
the creation, when the
clay begins to breathe.
Nothing is more exciting
than being nearby when
the breathing starts.

A
"promotion"
out of teaching

would give me
good money and real power.

But I already
have
good money—

good in the sense
that I don't have to do
anything bad to get it.

Hey, I get paid for doing what I enjoy most: reading books, talking with people who have read the same books, making discoveries, and asking questions like "What is the point of being rich, anyhow?" and "Are there other ways to define *rich*?" and "We hear angry talk about terrorists striking from across the seas, but does each of us have a terrorist in our own heart, striking us from within by telling us to be greedy for more money and more power?"

But wait.

I already have plenty of power.

I have the power
   to nudge,
   to fan sparks,
   to water parched roots,
   to ask troubling questions,
   to praise an attempted answer,
   to condemn hiding from the truth,
   to suggest books to read,
   to point to where a pathway starts.

What power is more real than asking questions like "What do you mean by *real*? Do you mean *real* as in *real estate* or as in *real world* or as in *royal*, one of the original forms of the word? If you found out that you were going to die next week, would it matter whether you were royalty? Incidentally, we are all, metaphorically speaking, going to die next week. What do I mean by *metaphorically* in that sentence?"

But teaching also
offers something
besides good money
and real power.

It offers love.

Not only the love of learning
and of books and of ideas,

but also the

love that a teacher feels for that real student
who walks into a teacher's life, begins to
breathe, and then walks out.

Perhaps

love

is the wrong word.

Is

magic

what I mean?